It's Showtime!

By
Rod Parsley

Columbus, Ohio

IT'S SHOWTIME!

TABLE OF CONTENTS

5

Chapter One

THE SPIRAL OF SILENCE

Many years ago, Napoleon Bonaparte summoned his generals to a council of war. While they were there, Napoleon walked over to a map that outlined a large country in red. "Here, gentlemen," he said, tracing the outline of that country with his finger, "lies a sleeping giant. If she ever harnesses her great natural resources with her manpower, let the whole world tremble. But she sleeps." He then held his finger to his pursed lips. "Shhh," he said quietly. "Let her sleep."

I have no doubt the devil has said the same thing about the church. I can imagine him among a gathering of his principal demons, looking at a profile of the body of Christ. He points to the church and hisses, "Here lies a sleeping giant. If she ever awakes to her authority and arises with the strength of multiplied millions who profess faith, let the hordes of hell tremble. But she sleeps." With a diabolical chuckle, he smiles and says, "Shhh! Let her sleep."

Through the ages, God has been sending His people wake-up calls by the mouths of His servants the prophets. In the same way we are tempted to hit the snooze buttons on our alarm clocks to find a few more minutes of sleep, we have disregarded the alarms God has sent us in His Word and sought solace in slumber. But unlike the clock at our bedside, God's alarm is one we can't turn off.

The Apostle Paul said it this way in Ephesians 5:14: "Awake, thou that sleepest, and arise from the dead, and Christ shall give thee light." He was paraphrasing the prophet Isaiah, who said in Isaiah 60:1, "Arise, shine; for thy light is come, and the glory of the Lord is risen upon thee."

Do you remember the last holiday meal you enjoyed with your family? Everyone brought some special dish to share, and everyone ate more than they should have. Afterward, everyone got sleepy, because slumber always accompanies overeating. How many times have you seen family members and friends sprawling and snoozing on the living room furniture while the television droned on?

Unfortunately, this has become a picture of the body of Christ. We have eaten the husks of the world until we are stuffed with them, and instead of fulfilling our purpose to set a world of captives free, we have become satisfied in our self indulgence and fallen asleep. Instead of regarding the nightly news as a warning that we have to work quickly and efficiently, we have allowed it to lull us into turning over for just a few more minutes of rest. How did we get into this sad condition, and what can be done about it?

Our adversary the devil has used two tactics with a great degree of success to keep the church silent when it should have been speaking, and in hiding when it should have been visible. One is intimidation, the other is deception.

First Peter 5:8 says, "Be sober, be vigilant; because your adversary the devil, as a roaring lion, walketh about, seeking whom he may devour..." A lion's roar can be a very intimidating thing, but the devil knows that he has no power at all over a child of God. The problem is that many believers don't know this, so the devil bluffs and blusters and causes many Christians to forfeit rights and privileges that God provided for them. The devil will try to make you fearful and make you flee through threats and false accusations, and he has been fabulously successful with this tactic.

The devil is also a deceiver. He will do his best to arrange every circumstance to appear as though you are falling and failing, and will try to steal everything God gave you when you regard your shifting circumstances. Fear will paralyze you, and condemnation will bind you, if you allow them to. Besides these things, the thief doesn't have to be strong; all he has to do is wait until nobody is home before he steals your goods.

The Bible says, "…be sober, be vigilant…." Both these words carry the idea of watchfulness and wakefulness, lest anyone deceive us or gain an advantage over us. The Word of God is indisputable; we need to wake up and be aware of the devil's devices.

When the alarm wakes you in the morning, chances are you don't just stay in bed the rest of the day. You get up and go about your regular routine, and do whatever you need to do. You take action. You move. You work. You speak.

The same thing needs to happen to us as believers. When we hear God's alarm, we can't just stay prostrate, wondering what that noise was that disturbed our slumber. We must arise. We have to get up. And once we're up, we can't just stand there yawning and scratching our heads, we have to take action. We have to move, and work, and speak. We are God's representatives, and we can't represent God by remaining sleepy-headed and bleary-eyed.

One of the dilemmas we face when we arise is that the very atmosphere around us is saturated with the messages of political correctness and cultural sensitivity that tell us to be quiet and not do or say anything that could be perceived as outside the mainstream. The message is quite clear: "Everybody's doing it, and you should be doing it, too," or, "Everybody thinks this way, and you should, too."

In the 1960s, Elisabeth Noelle-Neumann, a German researcher, conducted public opinion polls in her country, similar to many of the polls

9

we hear about in America today. Her findings led her to conclude that people have a tendency to speak more openly about their beliefs when they perceive that they hold a majority position. Those who feel their point of view is in the minority will be less likely to speak out. This has become known as the spiral of silence theory. Even though debate goes on in the academic community about the accuracy of the theory, it explains to me why the church has been silent in many areas where it should have been speaking.

As believers, many of the convictions we have and many of the values we hold are characterized in our culture as outside the mainstream. Television, movies, music, and print media all try to convince us that nobody feels the way we do, and our voices are not heard. We are told that what we believe doesn't matter, and that we are in the minority, so we need to be quiet and sit down. For many years, we believed that lie.

One of the main reasons we have been marginalized is because we have taken unspeakable glory and manifold cure and bungled our presentation. When we did have the opportunity to speak, we acted as though we needed to apologize for what we had to say, and said it with so little conviction that we convinced no one that our point of view was worth a second glance. The world has been lying well, while we have been telling the truth badly. Let me give you some examples.

When we do manage to persuade someone to come to church with us, what do they find when they get there? Do they see the love and the power of God in demonstration in such a way that they cannot deny that God Himself is in our midst? Or do they see a chromium-plated, fully synthesized, over-organized and artificial representation of a transcendent and almighty God?

It is a sad fact that at many churches the only place people see God is on the sign outside the building. God Himself told us about what kinds of things we should be able to expect wherever He has chosen to place His name. We read about it in the gospel of Mark, chapter 16. Here are three qualifications Jesus gave us, among others: "...they shall cast out devils; they shall speak with new tongues…they shall lay hands on the sick, and they shall recover."

Does this frighten you? Do these things sound too controversial for your liking? Why don't they do these things at your church? Why don't you do them yourself?

Let me make this even more personal. What is it your neighbors see in you that makes them want to be a Christian? Do you think they are ready to forsake a life that is meaningless just because you go to church on Sunday morning? When they hear statistics that indicate that divorce is as big a problem for church-going folks as it is for those who profess no church affiliation, what makes you think that you getting dressed up and driving away to a church building one morning a week is going to make a difference to them? Why in the world would they want to be a part of that?

When the unchurched see people all dressed up coming to the restaurant on Sunday afternoon, where do you suppose they think they're coming from? And how do you expect them to react when they see the so-called Christians complaining about the service, criticizing the food, and leaving no tip, just an outdated and discolored tract that says "Jesus Loves You"? Is it any wonder the church has become irrelevant to millions?

I don't know about you, but I don't want to be a part of something like that. I feel like going to some church parking lots while their services are under way, standing up on the hood of an automobile, and shouting at the top of my lungs, "Why do you bother?"

I don't want to be part of a parade, I want to be part of an army! We have not been called to show off our medals while we polish our armor. We have been called to go into battle for the hordes of humanity that are headed to hell unless someone stands in front of them and demonstrates to them there is a better way—a way that leads to life, not to death and destruction.

A Senator from Georgia pointed out the need to speak out some time ago. In a speech in the United States Senate entitled "A Deficit of Decency," Zell Miller said that in times like these, "...silence is not golden; it is yellow."

We must stand up to be seen and speak loud to be heard, and when we stand and speak, we must be ready for the scrutiny that is sure to follow. It won't be easy, but it will be necessary. Taking the easy way is what led us to the place we are in. There is a way out, but it will require boldness and courage on our part. Up to now there have been far too few voices for righteousness crying in the wilderness. It's time we took up the call and spread this message to the highways and the byways—from the halls of power in Washington, DC to the smallest village in the country; from the furthest reaches of the nation to the neighborhood where you live.

This is not a pipe dream, nor is it wishful thinking. This is the reality and the necessity of the present age. Men and women of God in years past saw what I am describing to you now and were awed at the glory of God's presence that would be manifested among His people.

During the healing revival of the 1940s and '50s, a world evangelist named Tommy Hicks went to Argentina and conducted a revival that shook that nation with the gospel. Afterward, God gave him a vision of what the body of Christ

would look like and accomplish in the last days—
the days in which we are now living.

In the vision, Brother Hicks was looking at the
earth from some height above it, and saw a great
giant asleep on the ground. The giant's body was
covered with debris, and when he tried to rise,
thousands of grotesque creatures would run away
from him. When he stopped struggling to get up
and became calm, the creatures would come back.

Suddenly the giant raised his hands toward
heaven, and all the hideous creatures fled into the
darkness. The giant managed to get to his feet, and
as he did, he raised his hands into the clouds. All
the debris and filth that clung to him disappeared.
Then the clouds became silver, and began to rain
upon the entire earth. The giant melted and literally became millions of people in all nations of
the world, lifting their hands and praising God.

Jesus appeared and stretched his hand out to
those who were praising Him, and He anointed
them for service. Many went forth to proclaim the
gospel, but many others refused the call of God,
and backed away from His presence. These were
swallowed up in darkness, while the others who

15

received light and life went everywhere, proclaiming the Word with signs and wonders following. No peril, pestilence, or persecution could stop them, and their testimony reached the ends of the earth, culminating in the rapture of the church.

What a picture of a triumphant and victorious church, doing the work of the Lord at the end of the age! And, my brothers and sisters, we are that church, and the end of the age is upon us. As someone once said, if these are not the last days, they are our only days, and we need to redeem the time, for the days are evil, and work the works of God while there is light. Time waits for no man, and the darkness is nearer than when we first believed. There are multitudes in the valley of decision, and we have the chance to reach them. We must not delay.

If this is an accurate picture of the end-time church as God envisions it, why have we had such a difficult time breaking out of the bonds of religious tradition and taking our rightful place as a glorious church without blemish? Why have we developed new forms which have bound us just as securely as the ones we left behind? How long will we be satisfied holding the fort until Jesus comes to get us out of the mess we got ourselves into? What are we hiding from in our sanctuaries—as though they were the only places of safety in a world full of danger?

I believe the real reason we have developed a siege mentality and have not successfully fulfilled the great commission is because we have turned inward instead of outward, and have become more self-centered than other-centered. We have become focused on I and me instead of on you and Him. We have become more interested in how many we have coming to our church services to get a blessing than how many we have going to our streets to be blessing. We would rather hold hands in our sanctuaries than lend a hand at the homeless shelters. We are proud of our designer outfits but are not clothed with humility. We drive big expensive automobiles but will not use them to bring anyone with us to church. We have purchased new houses in nice neighborhoods, but have no time to serve because we have to work two jobs to pay the mortgage.

Second Kings chapter 7 tells a fascinating story in the history of Israel that applies to our present situation. The Syrian army besieged the city of Samaria, the capitol of the northern kingdom of Israel. Food became so scarce that people were resorting to cannibalism. In the midst of the torment of the siege, God gave a word through the prophet Elisha that the famine would be broken and regular commerce would resume. God created such confusion in the enemy's camp that they fled in terror, leaving all their gear and provisions behind.

Four lepers came into the camp, and were shocked to find it deserted. They began to eat and drink, even plundering some of the tents and hiding the treasure they found in them. Then they remembered that the entire city was starving to death while they were enjoying abundance just outside the gates.

Second Kings 7:9 says, "Then said they one to another, 'We do not well: this day is a day of good tidings, and we hold our peace….'"

The gospel, or good news, must be made available to all. It is a day of good tidings, and if we hold our peace, we will surely be rightfully accused of "doing not well." How many souls are in hell because we refused to speak? How many are still suffering because we were afraid to tell them the good news we have taken for granted for so long?

In *Foxe's Book of Martyrs* there is the story of a Dutch widow named Wendelmuta who was imprisoned by the church for the crime of heresy, which in those days meant she was a true believer in Jesus. Before her sentence was pronounced she was visited by a friend of hers, who asked her why she would not recant her confession of Jesus Christ as Savior and just believe on Him secretly in her heart.

Wendelmuta replied, "Ah, you know not what you say. It is written, 'With the heart man believeth unto righteousness; and with the mouth confession is made unto salvation.'" (Romans 10:10) She was burned at the stake, and all her goods were confiscated as a result of her testimony of faith.

In times of persecution people would have their tongues cut out as a punishment for confessing faith in Christ. Today there are millions who claim to know Christ who have never shared their faith with one other person. What threat has made them hold their peace? Who cut out their tongues?

It's time to break the spiral of silence and speak about the Savior who brought us out of a life of sin and destruction and into a life of blessing and abundance. The message of the gospel was never meant to be hidden behind sanctuary walls or locked up in religious institutions. It was meant to be shouted from the housetops and published in the streets. Jesus died for us. We must live for Him. It's time to be silent no more.

4

Chapter Two

THE SILENCE IS BROKEN

A great deal of attention has been focused on special interest groups, especially those that are perceived as influencing public policy. It seems that every cause under the sun has one or more organizations devoted exclusively to promoting their specific interests and ideals. Many times different groups have opposing agendas, and they align themselves on opposite sides of virtually every issue. Ever escalating amounts of money and rhetoric are poured into every debate, and the stakes continue to climb higher and higher. Enormously expensive advertising campaigns cajole, insinuate, and even threaten. Dire warnings are issued, and impending doom is declared if a point of view is not accepted or a course of action is not pursued.

I am convinced the body of Christ is the largest special interest group in America. According to one poll, 85 percent of Americans claim to be Christians. If this is true, why don't we have more influence than we do? What politician would dare promote a piece of legislation if he knew 85 percent of his constituents were opposed to it? Yet a Christian perspective is seldom given a fair hearing in the public forum, and persecution of evangelical Christians has become an art form in some places in our society. Politicians are quick to curry the favor of believers at the ballot box, but then just as quickly forget about their promises to them when making deals in the back rooms of government buildings.

Historically, one of the problems we have seen is that Christians cannot agree on anything of substance. We may say we are in unity, but the camaraderie that seems to be generated at the inter-fellowship spaghetti dinner evaporates when someone stands up and says, "I have a plan to win souls in this city. Who wants to help me?"

This one can't agree with that one on an obscure point of doctrine. This one administers a sacrament differently than that one. This group baptizes by immersion. That group baptizes by sprinkling. This church plays contemporary music in their services. That church doesn't believe in musical instruments in their services. A bewildered world shrugs their shoulders and avoids the whole religious mess we have made, and we remain fragmented, separated from our parts, and powerless.

Unity means more than being able to sit down at the local cafeteria to part chicken bones with people from other churches. There are lots of people who do that, and they have just as much bitterness and resentment toward their fellows after they are done as they did before they started.

Unity does not mean I should have to forfeit my values to embrace a point of view that is contrary to my convictions. That is not unity, it is compromise. There are certain things about which we should not yield, but just because others do not agree with me in every area does not mean I cannot find common ground with them as we work together to see God's will accomplished.

During the years when nuclear energy was being developed for everything from bombs to power plants, some of the scientific terminology that explained the processes involved in nuclear physics found its way into general use. One of these terms is critical mass, which is defined as the smallest amount of fissionable material sufficient to sustain a nuclear chain reaction. Or, in the words of a junior high student in science class, "...you got to have enough stuff to make the thing go boom."

One of the things we have been missing in the body of Christ is critical mass—we haven't had enough stuff to cause an explosion, or even make much noise. We have allowed the things that divide us to be more important to us than the things that unite us—and as a result we have been helpless to prevent the moral decay and accelerating decline we have witnessed in our culture. We have allowed the devil's intimidation and deception and the spirit of sectarianism to keep us separated, rather than rising above the rifts that our religious rituals have caused and moving forward to proclaim the gospel to the ends of the earth.

But I see a shift coming.

The largest number of people focused on the smallest point of agreement yields the greatest results. I see people from every spectrum of Christianity coming together in agreement on issues that matter to them. They are standing together with one heart and one mind, and speaking with one voice as they confront critical matters of conscience. And with the help of the Holy Spirit, they are making a difference in this generation.

There was a time when pastors and church leaders would be intimidated by cultural forces that conspired to keep them bound. That time is over. Of course, there are still some who prefer the religious status quo, but there are many more who are shedding the shackles of dead, dry formalism and responding to the rain of the Spirit being poured out in these last days. These coura- geous men and women are not just informed about the Word of God, but also about the issues of the day, and they are not afraid to speak the truth with confidence and compassion.

Since the last presidential election, I have been interviewed on many of the major media outlets in the country, answering questions about everything from the sanctity of life to the suffering in the African nation of Sudan. Even though I have encountered some who will not receive the truth, for the most part I have found that a calm and reasoned response is well received, even about emotional issues such as abortion.

We must not shrink back from addressing these issues, because if there is ever a time that our voices need to be heard, it is now. We have abandoned the field for too long, and those who oppose us have been unopposed, and their voices have been the only ones heard in the marketplace of ideas. This must change, and is changing. I, for one, will be silent no more. Let me explain why.

First, our times demand it. We live in an hour where we spend millions to save the whales and the whooping cranes, yet destroy our own children. We build strong, stable houses, yet have weak, sick homes. We know more and understand less. We go faster and farther, but get nowhere. Our medical technology has become so advanced that we look forward to a longer life span than any generation in history, yet we use that same technology to try to create clones to be harvested like a commodity. We now have drug abusing mothers who put their next fix ahead of their child's next meal. We have fathers whose perverted drive for sexual gratification goes beyond their daughters' need for common dignity. Our passions have become riderless horses, plunging madly toward the abyss of anarchy.

I must speak because our history compels it. Regardless of the best efforts of the revisionists, history still records that the Founding Fathers were men of faith and vision. Their vision of America was not perfect, but it has stood the test of time, as well as the attacks of tyrants from without and treachery from within. The faith that enabled them to stand resolute in the face of insurmountable obstacles, and the faith that informed their vision was historic Christianity.

I must speak because our future requires it. Unless there is a repudiation of the monstrous cousins of materialism and humanism that have moved America to the status of a postmodern, and some say post-Christian nation, we will lose the inheritance passed on to us by the blood, tears, and treasure of our forefathers within one generation. For the past forty years there has been a widening gap between what we consider traditional values and the belief system of the young. If we refuse to defend what we say we hold dear, we are in danger of losing it altogether.

Finally, I must speak because God is watching. I feel like Paul, who said, "Woe unto me, if I preach not the gospel." There is a commission that commands me; a covenant that constrains me; a conviction that commits me to speaking the truth by every means available. This same commission is given not just to me, but to every one who names the name of Christ.

As I have traveled in my home state of Ohio and to the corners of the nation, I have been gratified to see that I am not the only one speaking out about these issues. There are multitudes who have been hidden, only to be revealed in this last day, that are coming out of the wilderness like

John the Baptist, not dependent on any man or group of men, but receiving their provision from the Lord. They are speaking with authority, and the world cannot resist the spirit and the wisdom with which they proclaim the truth. They truly have the spirit of a revolutionary. History is full of their examples.

Keep him cloistered in an Augustinian monastery, and Martin Luther will refute the dead dogma of organized religion and start a Reformation that reverberates worldwide.

Put a bounty on his head and force him into exile in a foreign land, and William Tyndale will print the first English language Bible, confirming his promise that a plowman would be able to have as much knowledge of the Scriptures as a priest.

Confine him to a Bedford prison for crimes against the religious rulers of his day, and John Bunyan will write the greatest literary work known to Christianity since the New Testament in *Pilgrim's Progress*.

A revolution can be defined as activity designed to overthrow the status quo and produce a fundamental change in the socioeconomic status of a group. We need such a revolution today.

Throughout the ages countries and kingdoms have been birthed on the battlefield of a revolutionary movement. These crusades have been championed by soldiers and citizens who refused to be denied, delayed or detoured in their quest to take up a cause they believed deserving of even death itself.

The effect of such an upheaval has been the escalation of every political, social and religious movement from communism to feminism, Marxism to Nazism, anarchy to democracy, mayhem to martyrdom.

A revolution becomes necessary when the virtue and intelligence or vice and ignorance of the people demand it. At that point, compromise and negotiation become void and revolution is inevitable.

The only way for evil to excel is for good men to do nothing. A church that professes to uphold the cause of Christ, yet condemns confrontation is nothing more than a social club that wants rain without thunder and lightning. They long to avoid confrontation by dwelling in the devil's demilitarized zone in order to preserve their facade of peace.

Power concedes nothing without a demand. The control of any dictator is established by the endurance of those whom he oppresses, and brave men negligent to their office are worth no more than cowards who desert their post during a time of danger.

We are at a point of crisis. Our culture is in chaos. The moral foundation once constructed by the tenets of our faith is quickly crumbling around us with no sign of a cure. We are at a crossroads— a strategic inflection point—and we are faced with a choice.

When complacency exceeds the desire for change, the consequence is concession and chaos. But when comfort and contentment no longer pacify the people, negotiations are terminated, talk is no longer tolerated and freedom at any cost becomes the catalyst for confrontation and change. The culture then begins to groan under the pressure of giving birth to a revolution—a culture shaking revival where the moral climate of our cities is changed and the effect is felt like shock waves across the nation.

At the birth of the infant church such a revival became apparent. Men and women became martyrs and misfits who were mocked and tortured by the religious elite, but like Shadrach, Meshach and Abednego, they did not bow and could not burn.

Today I see the same fire burning and a glorious church rising out of obscurity. I perceive a remnant who will gladly expend their lives for a cause greater than themselves.

There is no greater drama than the sight of remnant believers scorned by a succession of adversaries, bearing trials with tenacity, multiplying miraculously—building order in chaos, fighting the sword with the Word, savagery with hope, defeating their strongest adversary while rescuing the despondent, restoring the down-hearted and reviving the life of Christ in the hearts of humanity.

Though beaten and battered, they are propelled by a power greater than themselves. They are compelled by an inward desire to serve an infallible leader through irresistible power based on absolute truth. Men and women with such spiritual stock don't cave in under pressure.

Give me a leader:

Like David, who in the face of Goliath and the Philistine armies cried out, "Is there not a cause?"

Like Moses, who in the courts of Pharaoh declared, "Let my people go!"

Like Patrick Henry, who at the start of the American Revolution cried, "Is life so dear, or peace so sweet, as to be purchased at the price of chains and slavery? Forbid it, Almighty God! I know not what course others may take; but as for me, give me liberty, or give me death!"

Like Dr. Martin Luther King, Jr., who on the Washington Mall in the face of racial segregation preached, "Let freedom ring . . . from every village and every hamlet, from every state and every city. We will be able to speed up that day when all of God's children, black men and white men, Jews and Gentiles, Protestants and Catholics, will be able to join hands and sing in the words of that old Negro spiritual, "Free at last! Free at last! Thank God Almighty, we are free at last!"

This revolution is not for the timid or weak, but the strong and brave who have stepped over the line and out of the comfort zone—those who have decided to be disciples of Christ and no longer need preeminence, position or popularity.

The time has come to enlist in this revolutionary army, follow our orders, take up our arms, invade the corridors of the doomed and damned, engage our archenemy, Satan, and set this hell-bound generation free. Thrust in the sickle, and reap: for the harvest truly is ripe.

The eyes of the Lord are running to and fro for a remnant who will stand in the gap and make up the hedge for humanity. He is looking for some warriors who don't have to be right, recognized or rewarded—for these alone will reap the end time harvest of souls, and receive His eternal reward and righteous commendation.

I find it fascinating that the great leaders of generations past have always been men and women who have not only known how to harness the power of words, but have led by their example. It is no leader who waits until someone else steps forward to test the waters. Leaders lead—and they must be seen to be followed.

I believe there are three things that are necessary to cause revival to spread from God's leaders to multiplied millions of believers in this generation.

First, there must be word from the Lord spoken under a prophetic unction. This cannot be on the level of a verse from a promise book or some general maxim sought out as a result of a current crisis. This must be a fresh word from heaven that comes not from the calloused surface of mental reasoning, but from the fleshly tablets of a heart turned toward God. Amos 3:8 says, "The lion hath roared, who will not fear? The Lord God hath spoken, who can but prophesy?" When men speak because God has spoken, there is authority in their words.

Next, there must be a priesthood who will bring the people into God's presence. Too often when the word of the Lord is heard, it is treated about the same as the daily news. We need to respond as though our lives depended on it, because they do. Joel chapter 2 describes the urgency that should characterize a solemn assembly: "Blow the trumpet in Zion, sanctify a fast, call a solemn assembly: gather the people, sanctify the congregation, assemble the elders, gather the children…." (Joel 2:15-16) Everyone was needed, and no one was left out. Calling on the Lord during a time of solemn assembly was expected of everyone, not just the preachers or the church staff.

Third, there must be intercessors who are willing to declare the word God has given them back into the heavens in prayer. Much of our praying has devolved into a heavenly wish list. We must begin again to say what God has already said, and focus on what He wants done instead of only what we want Him to do. Isaiah 51:16 says, "And I have put my words in thy mouth, and I have covered thee in the shadow of mine hand, that I may plant the heavens, and lay the foundations of the earth, and say unto Zion, thou art my people."

When we declare what God has already spoken under a prophetic anointing as we gather in a solemn assembly, we will plant the heavens with the words God has given us, and lay the foundations of the earth. God's word will seed the heavenly realm as grains of wheat, and the word of the Lord will be established in us.

I am convinced this is where we have fallen short in the past. God has raised up anointed men and women who are proclaiming His word in power and authority. We have had solemn assemblies with music, preaching, drama, dance, and everything else we could think of, but there has been little emphasis on intercession. We say we have been waiting on God to move. I believe God has been waiting on us to put our fork down, push our plate back, and begin to speak what He has already proclaimed back to Him, so the foundations of the earth can be established.

In 2 Kings 2:14, Elisha was about to cross back over the Jordan River after Elijah's dramatic departure into heaven. Taking the mantle of Elijah that fell back to the earth, Elisha struck the waters of Jordan and said, "Where is the Lord God of Elijah?"

IT'S SHOWTIME!

I believe that today God is looking at the earth and saying, "Where are my Elijahs?" We are not waiting on God—He is waiting on us.

In Acts 5:20, when the apostles were jailed for preaching in the name of the Lord Jesus Christ, an angel came from heaven, supernaturally delivered them from their bonds, and said, "Go, stand, and speak in the temple to the people all the words of this life." They took the words God gave them and spoke them boldly both in private prayer and in public proclamation.

God forbid that we should have to be thrown in prison or receive an angelic visitation before we begin to do what Jesus has already commanded us to do. The grave is empty. Christ has risen. The silence is broken. Will you take your place among those who will "go, stand, and speak"?

3

THE TIME HAS COME

Not only was the November 2004 election an opportunity for the nation to choose its president for the next four years, but in my home state of Ohio voters had the chance to amend the state constitution to define marriage as the union of one man and one woman. I realized there was something I must do about the issue, but that realization had actually come many months before.

In November of 2003, I was privileged to be present when President Bush signed into law the Partial Birth Abortion Ban Act. I know I represented many other Americans who said this procedure should not be allowed in America, and I felt humbled to be a part of such a historic occasion. But as I looked around the room, I noticed that virtually everyone there was older than me. I wondered where all the people of my generation were, and what would happen when those who had stood so steadfastly against the tide of moral decline were gone. I knew then the time had come for action.

Ohio's marriage amendment was opposed by lawmakers, mayors, newspapers, corporations, and, it seemed, just about everyone who was anyone in the state. The amendment's supporters were challenged at every step in the process, including the struggle to even get it on the ballot. What could be done to overcome the forces arrayed against them?

In the summer of 2004 I was busy doing what God called me to do, overseeing five ministry outreaches, and had at that time recently started a sixth. I wasn't looking for something else to accomplish. I was planning for a major ministry event that is one of the two largest meetings we hold every year at our church. My schedule was packed for the rest of the year. Then God spoke.

If we do not allow ourselves to become sensitive to the Holy Spirit, we may find ourselves doing things out of a sense of rote or routine instead of being inspired and moved by the hand of God. Human beings have a way of becoming comfortable with what is familiar, and anything that upsets their regular schedule is regarded with suspicion.

Consider your own life. If you are like most people, you go through the same routine every day, even down to the way you brush your teeth and put on your clothes. You probably drive to work the same way, eat lunch at the same place, and order the same things from the menu.

Think about your relationship with God. Do you talk to God as though you were having a conversation with a close friend, or is your prayer life filled with memorized phrases or slogans that you heard someone else say? Do you really mean it when you toss off a sentence or two toward heaven before you fall in bed exhausted? Do you go to church with the attitude that this might be the day your life changes forever, or are you looking forward to getting back home so you can take your Sunday afternoon nap?

This resistance to change is not only true for individuals, but for churches and religious organizations as well. Someone once said that if the Holy Spirit was removed from the earth, eighty percent or more of church work would go on as usual. The routines we follow are not necessarily sinful, but we must guard against complacency, which will lead us to the place where we feel we do not need God's guidance any longer.

I will never forget the day I walked from my office to another part of the building, and found myself curled up in a fetal position in the hallway with my head under a chair, sobbing and shaking under the power of God. In that moment, God asked me a question.

It's one thing for you to ask God a question, but it is another matter altogether when God asks you a question. After all, it's not as though He is asking you something He does not already know. He is not coming to you for counsel, He is trying to teach you something, so when God inquires, wait for the answer.

Every time I think about this, I am reminded of the first time I met Dr. Lester Sumrall. He conducted a service in our little 280-seat building, and afterward as we were sitting down at a local restaurant I apologized to him that our church was so crowded. People were literally sitting on top of other people, and we had to set up his book table outside the building, where the wind blew the tables over and scattered his books all over the parking lot.

"I'm so sorry," I said. "We certainly want to have you back, but I just need to get more faith so we can have a bigger building when we invite you again."

He looked across the table with those piercing blue eyes and said, "You don't need more faith, you just need to know what faith is." He paused and then said, "Would you like me to tell you?"

At this point, I didn't start quoting Mark 11:22-24, or spouting off some theological premise that I had learned in Bible College. I was sitting across the table from a man who was casting out devils in the mountains of Tibet long before I was born. I was young and there was a lot I didn't know, but I did know enough to hold my peace and listen to what this man of God had to say to me about faith. I leaned across the table so far that my tie fell into my food.

"Faith," Dr. Sumrall said, "is knowing God."

I have taken the simple truth of that statement and used it virtually every day. I knew when God asked me a question that day on the hallway floor, He did not expect me to answer—He expected me to listen.

"Why do you do what you do?" God said to me. "Why do you have this building? Why do you have a staff? Why do you have church services? Why do you have an automobile, or an airplane, or a suit of clothes?"

I couldn't move, and couldn't respond. I was waiting for the answer, and God spoke again.

"The apex of all Christian endeavor must become to place the jewel of a soul in the crown of the Savior."

This profound precept has guided everything I have done since then. I found myself examining all my efforts against its potential to bring souls into the kingdom. If it didn't result in men and women being saved, I looked at it completely differently than before. And when God spoke to me to do a thing, I responded immediately, even when it didn't make sense to my natural mind.

In August of 2004, God spoke again. He told me to cancel my ministry meetings, including our annual Pastors' and Church Leaders' conference, and instead arrange meetings throughout the state of Ohio and elsewhere to talk about the need to protect marriage and restore America to traditional values. It was a dramatic change, but my heart had already been prepared.

As we began to make arrangements for these meetings, I was amazed at how quickly all the necessary details came together. Usually meetings like these required months of preparation, and we only had a few weeks. I met people I had never known before, and found help from places I would have never expected.

As I toured my home state as well as other major cities in America, I made the case for protecting marriage to as many people as would listen. And in place after place, it seemed as though I could see the scales falling from people's eyes as they understood the cost of sitting on the sidelines while the political process went on without them. They "got it".

On the eve of the election, I sensed that values voters were going to do something historic. I wasn't disappointed. Every state that had a ballot issue protecting marriage passed it by a large margin. In Ohio, it passed with 62 percent of the vote. The phenomenon of the values voter was a main topic of discussion for weeks after the ballots were cast. Overnight, it seemed, people of faith were the center of attention.

Ohio, especially, was considered the ultimate battleground state in the presidential election. For weeks, media scrutiny had been more intense than I had ever seen it before. On election night, the last state everyone was talking about was Ohio, and once the results from the Buckeye State were announced, it was all over. I believe this, too, was God's doing. We had asked for this moment, and now the spotlight of the nation's attention was on us. What would we do with it?

There are many examples in the Old Testament of those who found themselves in leadership positions representing a multitude of others whose lives literally depended on them. I want to point out two of them.

"Moses my servant is dead," God said to Joshua. "Now therefore arise, go over this Jordan, thou, and all this people, unto the land which I do give to them, even to the children of Israel." (Joshua 1:2)

What a tremendous responsibility Joshua carried over the Jordan River with him! Moses, the great lawgiver of Israel with whom God Himself spoke face to face was gone, and the eyes of all Israel were on Joshua to see what he would do. No doubt he felt inadequate for the task ahead of him, but it was not as though he was unprepared. What God was asking Joshua to do was stand in His presence so the glory of the Lord could be revealed in him. As they prepared to pass over the Jordan, God said in Joshua 3:7: "This day will I begin to magnify thee in the sight of all Israel, that they may know that, as I was with Moses, so I will be with thee."

When God calls you to accomplish a task, He will not only provide supernatural preparation, He will also give you supernatural help. If the only challenges you ever face are those you can do without God's help, why would you ever call upon Him? Here we see the plan of God unfolding, not only for Joshua and his generation, but for us in this generation. He has been preparing us for the positions of leadership He now expects us to take in these perilous times.

The tests Joshua faced after Israel's dramatic river crossing were immediate and imposing. Even after the formidable walls of Jericho came down, Joshua then had to deal with treachery in the camp. When the sin that held them back was dealt with, Joshua went on to lead the armies of Israel to victory after victory over their adversaries. In two sweeping campaigns involving 31 cities, Joshua's conquests paved the way for Israel's occupation of their land of promise.

Remember that Joshua was born as a slave in Egypt, and his only expectation was a life of slavery, where nothing, not even his physical strength, was regarded as his own. But many years later, when he stepped out of Moses' shadow, he stood up under scrutiny and fulfilled the purpose for which God created him. He is still considered one of the greatest military heroes in Israel's history. His moment came, and he stood resolutely in the spotlight and led his people into their promised land.

There is another example of preparation and prominence found elsewhere in the Old Testament in completely different circumstances. A young orphan girl among the captives of Israel was raised in a foreign land by her older cousin. She was like so many other captives—separated from her parents and her native land. What hope was there for her to become anything but a slave? She was unremarkable in every way, except for her physical beauty, but many pretty girls became old and haggard before their time in their struggle for subsistence in a strange country. Her name was Hadassah.

This young Jewish maiden had no idea what was in store for her, but God had a plan to bring her to the forefront and enable her to have a leading role in a drama that reached the furthest province of the Persian Empire.

After Queen Vashti was deposed for refusing to obey a royal decree, a beauty pageant was held across Persia to find a replacement. Hadassah, who was also known as Esther, was chosen to be among the many young women who were assembled in the palace. She was eventually selected by the king to be his new queen. But sinister forces were already at work planning the demise of all the exiled Jews. Esther's cousin, Mordecai, urged her to speak to the king about the matter, but Esther responded that nobody was allowed into the king's presence without a royal summons. Mordecai's response was compelling.

"For if thou altogether holdest thy peace at this time, then shall there enlargement and deliverance arise to the Jews from another place; but thou and thy father's house shall be destroyed: and who knoweth whether thou art come to the kingdom for such a time as this?" (Esther 4:14)

Esther realized her time had come, and she went in to the king unbidden. The scrutiny of the entire court was upon her as she stood under the king's gaze, but she remained steadfast in the spotlight. Esther was not only accepted in the monarch's presence, but given royal favor. She could have had anything she wanted, but she did not ask for a new wardrobe or another trinket to wear around her neck. She asked for the lives of her people to be spared. Help and deliverance came because someone was willing to go, and stand, and speak.

You may consider yourself a person without means. You may not be educated, or wealthy, or well connected. It may seem as though God should use anybody but you. There may be a thousand or more who are better qualified for the task God has asked you to undertake, but there you are—reluctantly thrust onto the stage. Your time has come. How will you respond?

Consider Paul's words in 1 Corinthians 1:26-29: "For ye see your calling, brethren, how that not many wise men after the flesh, not many noble, are called: but God hath chosen the foolish things of the world to confound the wise; and God hath chosen the weak things of the world to confound the things which are mighty; and base things of the world, and things which are despised, hath God chosen, yea, and things which are not, to bring to nought things that are; that no flesh should glory in His presence."

Keep this in mind at all times: When God asks you to do something in His name, it is not about you, it is about Him. He alone can qualify the unqualified for the tasks He chooses. If we say our lives are in His hands, why should we complain when He uses us as He wishes?

There are risks as well as rewards involved in every decision we make. While we usually think of what the consequences will be if we take some action, many times we disregard what conesquences will befall if we refuse to take action.

What if Joshua had not stepped forward after Moses died? What if he had said, "I've been Moses' understudy for forty years, and I still don't have anything to call my own. I quit." Not only would Joshua have missed his inheritance, an entire generation would have been in jeopardy.

What if Esther had refused to risk appearing before the king without being asked? Mordecai made it plain—she and her lineage would have been destroyed, and she would have placed all her countrymen in peril of death.

Psalm 24:6 says, "This is the generation of them that seek him, that seek thy face, O Jacob."

God is not waiting for someone else or for another generation to arise. Now is the time. This is the place. The day of the Lord is at hand. We must seek Him as never before, because the time is short and the need is great.

Lest you become weary and faint in your minds, let me explain what it is that we will find when we seek God's face. What kind of supernatural help is available from Him when we do as He asks?

I have never understood people who say God doesn't answer prayer. I have never read in my Bible where God turned a deaf ear to the cry of His children. The Bible says that God is a rewarder of them that diligently seek Him. There are three things serious seekers will find when they seek the face of God.

There are many noteworthy features about God's face, but the one I want to emphasize to you is His mouth. Here are the things that we receive from His mouth when we seek His face in prayer.

First, one of the most prominent features of anyone's mouth is their lips. The thing we receive from God's lips is His word. God's words framed the universe, fixed the stars in their sockets, sprinkled sand around the sea shore, gave Adam all the direction he needed to rule on the earth under God, raised the three day dead Prince of

God from the tomb, and gave you eternal life when you deserved eternal damnation. If God's word can do all this, it can fix whatever situation you are facing right now.

You don't need just any word; you need a word spoken under the anointing of the Holy Ghost. You can't expect to flip your Bible open to any passage and receive the word you need for the desperate straits you are in. You need a word spoken under the anointing that comes under an unction from heaven's holy pavilions.

Next, when you seek God's face, you will find His breath, which represents His Spirit. The word of God itself will be no more than black ink on white pages unless it is breathed upon by the Holy Ghost. It is the Spirit that gives life and vitality to everything God says. You will never gain the impetus you need to overcome obstacles in your way if the Bible never becomes more inspirational than the daily newspaper, but when the Spirit makes the Word real, nothing is impossible to you.

Third, when we seek God's face we will find His smile, which is His favor. God's favor is what will cause doors to open for you that have been slammed in your face. It is what will cause the banker to say "yes" when every time before the answer has been "no." Favor will cause you to rise up when you should have been pushed back, and will enable you to prevail instead of fail. God's favor upon you will lift you up when others are trying to cast you down. One smile from heaven will do more for you than the applause of millions on earth. Here's the wonderful thing about favor—it's not something you're going to get—it's something you already have as a result of seeking His face.

All these things that will propel you to victory—God's word, His Spirit, and His favor—are available to you now, at this moment. All you have to do is seek His face.

Will you follow the example of Joshua, Esther, and countless others throughout history, and step into the spotlight that is shining on the world's stage? Wouldn't you rather be regarded as a hero of faith instead of a historical footnote? The time has come. It's your time to shine. Let the glory of the Lord be revealed in you.

2

Chapter Four

THE TABLE IS SPREAD

Someone once showed me a picture of a long stretch of highway with freshly painted yellow lines right down the middle. Stretched out in the center of the road was a dead opossum with big yellow stripes sprayed over its bloated belly. The caption read, "It's not my job." Apparently nobody on the road crew had enough of a sense of responsibility to remove the carcass from the center line, so they just painted right over it.

We live in a world where we loudly claim our rights, but quietly forsake our responsibilities. We have become convenience oriented instead of commitment oriented. Instead of making decisions based on what is best for others, we only consider what is best for ourselves. Instead of making our lives better, this focus on self to the exclusion of others has resulted in our becoming more anxious, afraid, and angst-ridden than ever before.

Is there any hope for reformation before this generation implodes from the weight of its corruption? Many who have noticed these alarming and accelerating trends are quick to answer no. I have a different view, but it is not the viewpoint of an unrealistic optimist. My answer to the difficulties of the age is informed by the Word of God.

Psalm 24:6 says, "This is the generation of them that seek him, that seek thy face, O Jacob." I have already rehearsed the three things we find when we seek God's face. I'm going to continue to evaluate the characteristics of the generation described in this verse.

Let me make it clear that God is not excluding anyone because of their age. When the Bible says "this is the generation," it does not mean those of a specific age group. It means His people who are alive on the earth right now, at the end of the age. This is the generation destined to receive experiential revelation and manifestation of the glory of God.

In the gospel of John, chapter 2, Jesus and His disciples were invited to a wedding in the village of Cana in Galilee. As you know, this was when Jesus turned water into wine, which was the first of the many miracles that occurred during His public ministry. The governor of the feast was amazed when he tasted the wine. He told the bridegroom that most people served the best wine first, but he had saved the best for last.

God has done the same thing, because He has saved the best for last. This principle is true naturally and spiritually. When I played basketball, the coach would always keep track of how many fouls his players had. If someone accumulated too many fouls too early in the game, the coach would take him out for a period of time. One of the reasons for this was he always wanted his best players on the floor at the end of the game, especially if the game was close.

The clock is running, and the end is near. For multitudes who are still in the valley of decision, the outcome could go either way. Whether they win or lose in eternal life depends upon how we play the game.

Psalm 24:6 goes on to say we are to seek His face. This word seek literally means to follow after or diligently inquire about. This means more than just a casual glance or a half-hearted question. Diligence involves persistent and consistent inquiry that results in an answer. The only way we are going to be diligent in our asking is if we are inquiring about the things that really matter to us. Those who are uncertain or ambivalent seldom give their best effort. We will never pursue God's will diligently if we are not convinced of what it is. Essentially, I believe God is saying, "What do you want?"

We must be careful here to distinguish our heartfelt desires from our whims and wishes. Here's the way I like to characterize what you really want—what is it that you can't live without? What is it that keeps you up and makes you walk the floor at night? If you really desire it, you will pursue it, because the proof of desire is pursuit.

Let me ask the question another way—what is it we should be pursuing? If we are supposed to be examples of the character of Christ, we should desire the same things He desired. What do we see

Him saying to His Father in prayer? In the garden of Gethsemane, He prayed, "…not my will, but thine be done." And what is God's will for us in this final generation in the last act of human history? Psalm 2:8 says, "Ask of me, and I shall give thee the heathen for thine inheritance…."

Jesus lived His life so that God would be glorified. His purpose was not to be ministered unto, but to minister, and to give His life as a ransom for many. I'm not saying that we have to be martyred to do the will of God, but we could follow Jesus' example more closely by living for others instead of for self. Until we come to the point where we can put our own will to death, we will never experience the fullness of life that God has for us.

Jacob discovered this when he was alone the night before meeting his brother Esau after returning to Canaan from his exile in Mesopotamia. The Bible says a man met him there and wrestled with him all night. It was not until Jacob came to the end of himself that God changed his name from Jacob, meaning deceiver, to Israel, meaning a prince with God. His heavenly name change and attendant change in character came not because of his own strength, but in spite of it.

When we seek God's face, not for what we can get out of Him, but what we can do for Him, then we are ready to represent Him to the world that so desperately needs to see Him for who He really is. It is at this point, where our own plans and schemes do not matter to us any longer, that His glory is ready to shine through us to a lost and darkened world. In fact, God is looking for those who will do so.

Second Chronicles 16:9 says, "For the eyes of the Lord run to and fro throughout the whole earth, to show himself strong on behalf of them whose heart is perfect toward him." If your heart is to do what He wants, regardless of what you want, God is looking for you, and will perform mighty acts on your behalf. We are not waiting on God, He is waiting on us. Romans 8:19 declares that the entire creation is groaning in travail in anticipation of the revelation of the sons of God— those who act like Him, think like Him, walk like Him, and talk like Him.

We are that generation, and it is time for us to take our place and reveal God's glory. The multitudes that are in bondage are waiting to be set free. The nations that dwell in darkness are waiting for the light to shine so they can see the truth. We are the sons of God that the Bible refers to in Romans 8:19. This scripture is not talking about someone else, it's talking about you.

In Ezekiel chapter 3, God reminds the prophet that he has a responsibility as a watchman over the house of Israel. His job is to warn the wicked to forsake his wickedness and repent. If he fails to warn them, the blood of the unrighteous will be on his hands.

This scripture was made abundantly clear to Dr. Lester Sumrall when he was a young itinerant preacher. One night in the middle of a service, God gave him an open vision. He saw men and women of every nationality trotting down the road of life, unconcerned about their destiny. Then, in an in instant, they fell over a precipice and into the billowing flames of hell. As he recoiled from the sight, God said to him, "You're responsible!"

"Oh, no, Lord," Dr. Sumrall said. "I'm not responsible. I've never been to those places. I don't know those people—I've never seen them before."

It was then that God made Ezekiel 3 real to him, and placed within him a divine desire to go that fueled his ministry for the rest of his life.

Even though your call may not involve the entire world, as Dr. Sumrall's did, it does involve your part of it. You may not be called to go to the nations, but you are called to go somewhere, if only across the street to that neighbor who is lost and undone without God. It is imperative that you understand you are involved in something bigger than yourself.

Abraham was talking to God, and complaining that he had not as yet had any offspring. I am sure he was thinking in terms of a large family, which would have been customary for a patriarch in those days. Abraham was wondering if one of his servants would be his heir. Genesis 15:5 says, "And he (God) brought him (Abraham) forth abroad, and said, "Look now toward heaven, and tell the stars, if thou be able to number them: and he said unto him, so shall thy seed be."

God had to get Abraham out of his tent and under the canopy of heaven so he could get an idea of the greatness of God's promise to him. Abraham had been looking at the circumstances, and God wanted him to look at the possibilities. He had to look up to see the magnitude of the word given to him. It was as limitless as the sky.

What you have been looking at is very likely far less than the promise God has for you. We must get out of out tents—our tabernacles—our sanctuaries, and under the open heaven. God wants us to be a people of infinite possibility. Those who spend all their time looking at their feet never view distant horizons, but those who have seen the vistas of mighty mountains will never again be satisfied with the molehills in their backyard. The chicken spends his life looking at the ground, but God created you to be a person who, like the eagle, looks to the heavens. Instead of running and hiding when the storm comes, the eagle mounts up and allows the fierce winds to propel him higher and farther than he could have flown without them.

There are many who have said they could never do anything or become anything great for God, but they disregard the greatness of the need as well as the greatness of our God. You don't have to have the calling of a world evangelist to take the gospel to your next door neighbor, but you may be just the deliverer they need to break the chains that have kept them bound for generations. Peter put it this way on the day of Pentecost in Acts 2:39: "...For the promise is unto you, and to your children, and to all that are afar off, even as many as the Lord our God shall call." God is calling. Will you be among the multitudes who are responding?

Psalm 24:3 says, "Who shall ascend the hill of the Lord? Or who shall stand in his holy place?" These questions deserve some additional scrutiny.

God has historically met with men on top of mountains. This should come as no surprise, since God is high and lifted up, so His glory can be seen from afar. But God has never desired to be separated from His people. Only after Adam sinned in the garden was God restricted from communing personally with the man that He created. Eventually, He prescribed a sacrificial system that would allow men's sins to be covered by a substitute. It was temporary, but signified something better that was to come. From time to time, God would invite people into His awesome presence.

Who can forget the image of Moses ascending the mountain to receive the Law from God's hand? It was a sight that made him fear and tremble, yet Moses went up to speak personally with the God of all flesh. When he returned, his countenance reflected so much of the glory of God that he had to put a veil over his face.

Elijah was instructed by God to summon all Israel to Mt. Carmel. It was there that the true and living God discredited the false gods worshipped by the people and destroyed their false prophets. You remember the story—the idols gave no answer to the cries of their priests, but the God of Israel answered Elijah by fire, and the flames consumed the sacrifice and everything around it.

Jesus took three of His disciples with Him to the mount of transfiguration. While they were there, a bright cloud of God's glory overcame them, and Jesus was revealed as the blindingly brilliant Son of God. Other than Peter's babbling, the disciples were speechless at this spectacle.

Who shall ascend the hill of the Lord? Who will prevail against the outward challenge that comes with the summons to come up to God's holy hill, to meet with Him and commune with Him? You see, the devil won't leave you alone just because God's word has been heard in your heart. Trouble may try you. Calamity may come calling. Sleepless nights may stalk you.

Who shall ascend? How can they see the way when their eyes are full of tears? Who can take another step when their backs are bowed? Who can continue the climb when their hearts are broken? How can they keep on when their friends walk away without a word of explanation? Who can go higher when there is pressure everywhere, when trouble has become a constant and unwelcome visitor, and when peril stalks their steps?

It's you, my friend. You are the one God is talking about here. He did not make a mistake when He put His hand on you, and He has not forgotten the promise He made to you. Keep on climbing. Trouble may last for a night, but joy comes in the morning as you reach your destination.

Then, once the climb has been made, who shall stand in His holy place? Who will persevere against the inward scrutiny that inevitably takes place when man is pinned under the Almighty's piercing gaze? Keep in mind what happened to those in the Bible who received a visitation of God in all his glory. Job repented in dust and ashes. Isaiah said, "Woe is me, for I am undone!" Ezekiel fell upon his face. Daniel had no strength left in him. Peter cried, "Depart from me; for I am a sinful man, O Lord." Saul of Tarsus was knocked down and temporarily blinded. John fell at His feet as though dead.

Who shall stand in the holy place? Not those whose hearts and hands are turned toward selfishness and greed, nor those who have not forgiven their brothers, nor those who have spread lies and gossip about those around them. The Bible goes on in Psalm 24:4 to give us the characteristics of those who are able to stand in His glorious presence: "He that hath clean hands, and a pure heart; who hath not lifted up his soul unto vanity, nor sworn deceitfully."

It seems clear that God is looking for people who desire a change inwardly, in their hearts. These are they who are willing to be transformed from the inside out by the life of God that compels from within, rather than the rudiments of religion that constrain from without. God is looking for people who love Him and obey Him because of an inward desire, not because of the promise of reward or the threat of punishment—those who love Him because of who He is, not just for what He has or because of what He can do. He desires a people who won't run from His presence after they have received a blessing that pacifies their flesh, but before they have undergone a change that reflects His heart.

In this last hour of human history, God is birthing a people who will not run when trouble comes, but who will stand boldly, defending their inheritance from the forces of darkness. Our armor prophesies a conflict, and warns us that there is danger ahead. We should not be surprised when we hear the rumors of war, because we are in a war zone. The weapons of our warfare are not bombs and missiles, but words and deeds inspired and energized by the Holy Ghost.

We are built for this battle and we are created for this conflict; we will not bow and we cannot burn.

The Bible has several striking references to warfare when it describes the Christian life. A familiar passage is found in Ephesians 6, where Paul describes the armor of God, including the sword of the Spirit, which is the word of God. First Timothy 1:18 talks about "…warring a good warfare…" according to "…the prophecies which went before on thee…."

This warfare is not a contest in which the end is still in doubt. Victory has already been won, and the end is already assured. One of the statements Jesus made from the cross was, "It is finished." This was not the pathetic gasp of a disillusioned man who was witnessing the death of a dream. It was the triumphant cry of a conqueror who saw that the tide of battle had turned and complete and absolute victory was the only possible outcome.

Psalm 23:5 says, "Thou preparest a table for me in the presence of mine enemies...." The table has already been spread. Those who count themselves as your enemies are not dead, nor have they disappeared, but the proof of the completeness of your victory over them is that you can refresh yourself even in their presence, because you recognize they are no threat to you.

God is giving birth to a generation of people who will not faint or fall away, but who will persevere and prevail. Take your rightful place among the ranks of those who are demonstrating the adversary's defeat and ushering in the appearing of the Lord of glory.

1

Chapter Five

THE STAGE IS SET

President Harry Truman was faced with a dilemma, and called for one of his most trusted economic advisers to help him make an important decision. The economist said, "Well, on the one hand, you could do this, but on the other hand, you could do that." When Truman rehearsed the matter to one of his friends, they asked him what he did. "I asked for a one-handed economist," he replied.

With today's emphasis on values clarification and situational ethics, it seems as though every situation has more than one acceptable outcome. The world says there are no more absolute standards; no clear distinction between black and white. Every decision should be based on what you feel or what you think. Objective truth is no longer a viable concept. The Bible says that during certain periods of Israel's history, every man did that which was right in his own eyes—but instead of leading to freedom, that philosophy only resulted in anarchy and eventually bondage.

Proverbs 14:12 says, "There is a way which seemeth right unto a man, but the end thereof are the ways of death." In contrast, in Psalm 23:3 the psalmist thanks the Lord because He "...leadeth me in the paths of righteousness for his name's sake." What this indicates to me is that whatever action we take needs to be directed by God and not by our own reasoning or intellect. There are any number of things we could choose, but it is only when we choose to do the things God has directed us to do that we will see world changing results.

So what is it that God is asking us to do? We find one thing in Psalm 22:30: "A seed shall serve him; it shall be accounted to the Lord for a generation." Psalm 22 is a Messianic psalm attributed to David. In it, David graphically portrays the agony that the Messiah will suffer, and describes in detail death by crucifixion, hundreds of years before it was practiced in Palestine. But as the psalm comes to a close, David makes this statement about a seed, not just referring to the Messiah, but also referring to those who would come and declare God's righteousness to a people who were not yet born.

A seed is the chosen, set aside, and designated part of a harvest. When immigrants came to this country, they would carefully select the very best of their seed from a previous harvest to take with them to new fields. They wanted to make sure their crop in a new land would have the very best possible chance for success. They spared no effort to make sure the seed they chose was the remnant of grain that was most likely to produce. The chosen seed was one out of a hundred, or even one out of a thousand—carefully examined and hand picked.

God has chosen you as one among a multitude to be used in this last act of human drama being played out on the world's stage. His hand is upon you because you are the one He has picked to bring forth a harvest in this end time. It is a glorious and gratifying thing to know you are one of God's chosen vessels to bring revival to the earth.

But before you start rejoicing, let me explain what is necessary to bring forth a harvest.

In John 12:24, Jesus said, "Except a corn of wheat fall into the ground and die, it abideth alone: but if it die, it bringeth forth much fruit." First comes the planting, then comes the dying, then comes the harvest. This is an immutable principle that we see throughout the Bible.

Here we have an opportunity to find out whether we really mean what we say when we ask God for a harvest, because there can be no harvest without a death, and there can be no death without a planting, and there can be no planting without a seed. What we must realize is that when we ask God for a harvest, we are really asking God for a death by planting. This is contrary to our fleshly nature, since we are naturally programmed to prolong our lives. But we must remember that when we became born again, we chose God's way and not our own way.

In Israel, nearly everyone was connected to farming in some way, so this language used images they readily understood. In modern culture, we are much further removed from agriculture, so these terms may not be as familiar to us, but the concept has not changed. Let me explain three purposes for a seed.

First, a seed is born to die. It will never fulfill its purpose unless it does. I still remember my relatives talking about seed potatoes. These were remnants of the previous summer's harvest that were set aside to provide the basis for next year's crop. By the time they were planted, they didn't look like much—dry, twisted, and shriveled. But there was something in them that would not be denied, and when given the right conditions, they would spring up into new and flourishing potato plants. The seed that was planted might only be a very small part of a potato, but the result of its death would be an abundant harvest.

Jesus said in John 18:37, "To this end was I born…." He came to the world to be a sacrifice, and to offer His life as a payment for those held captive by the devil. He did not come to live for Himself; to indulge in the pleasures that this world had to offer. He came to adorn a cross—to be rejected and vilified by those He came to save;

and through His death He produced a perpetual harvest.

He instructed anyone who would follow Him to "...deny himself, and take up his cross, and follow me." (Matthew 16:24) There was a cross for Jesus, and if you will follow Him, there is a cross for you. You are not required to bear His cross, but you are required to bear yours—that is, if you care about producing a harvest.

Paul understood this when he said to the church at Galatia, "I am crucified with Christ: nevertheless I live; yet not I, but Christ liveth in me: and the life which I now live in the flesh I live by the faith of the Son of God, who loved me, and gave himself for me." He had literally come to the point where he realized his life was not his own, but he was fully and completely owned by the One who paid to redeem him.

In Matthew 20:28, Jesus said, "Even as the Son of man came not to be ministered unto, but to minister, and to give his life a ransom for many." Even though men worshipped Him, His purpose was not to be served but to serve others by laying down His life. If we believe our purpose ought to reflect His, how can we do any less?

For many church-goers, Christianity has become nothing more than a means by which they try to persuade God to give them the things they think they need to please their flesh, to inflate their ego, or to bolster their reputation or social standing. A postmodern and humanistic world view has actually convinced many that God exists for the express purpose of making us happy. And according to materialism, what should make us happy is an accumulation of material things. Multitudes of people have lived for years searching for the happiness they thought things could provide, and have become disillusioned and despondent when the things they possessed did not produce what they promised.

Let me put it very simply: self-sacrifice is entry level Christianity. It's not about me, it's about Him. It's not what I want, it's what He wants. It is not a matter of what I choose to do, it is a matter of what He has already chosen for me to do. This fundamental principle is lacking in many who claim Christ as Savior, and is one of the reasons the church is powerless to produce the harvest of souls that God requires. The seed has to be sacrificed in order to see the harvest come.

In order for a seed to die, it has to be planted. The planting is significant for a number of reasons. Planting means the seed gets buried. When a field is planted, nobody sees the seed any longer. This is hard for some who always want to be in the spotlight, but the seed's power is only released in secret.

Next, the seed is broken open. What is in the seed that is protected by its covering is released when the soil breaks down the outer shell to unlock what is inside. If the seed was never planted, it would not have the opportunity to undergo the necessary changes for a harvest to come forth.

In our case, death is always followed by burial. As a seed, when we are covered, dramatic changes can take place through the agency of the Holy Spirit that will result in a new life that will cause transformation in the lives of those around us.

It is the seed's responsibility to die and to be buried. It is the soil's responsibility to surround and sustain the seed in an atmosphere that is favorable to that seed breaking open and reproducing. Without the right kind of soil, even the best seed cannot reproduce. But when the conditions are right, a seed properly planted can bring forth even a hundredfold.

What is the soil that an individual believer should seek to be planted into? The right kind of environment that should receive believers as seeds and allow them to grow and flourish is a local church. Just as the seed will never develop its potential until it is planted, so Christians will never develop their potential unless they find fellowship in a local church.

I know there are a variety of excuses people have for not fellowshipping with one another in a local body of believers. I think I have heard them all. The fact remains that Jesus, our example, was found in the synagogue on meeting days, as was His custom. He was not always well received. There were even occasions where everyone there wanted to stone Him, but that didn't keep Him from assembling with His fellow worshippers.

The local church is to an individual believer what the soil is to the seed. It provides an atmosphere for growth and development that cannot happen otherwise. I know there will be challenges and the potential for misunderstandings, but that is all part of the dying process that is inevitable in order for us to bring forth new life. One of the reasons we have not brought forth the harvest God has ordained is because of our failure to put aside differences and hurts of the past and allow ourselves to die to what we want so we can produce what God wants. Dying can be painful, but it is necessary, and will happen if we allow ourselves to get planted.

Third, the seed is born to give life. Producing new life is a process, not a singular event. But if we allow God to take us through the process, life will follow death just as certainly as dawn follows darkness.

One of the most fascinating characteristics of seed is that each seed has life in itself. You may not realize it, but once you are born again you have the life of God in you. You are destined to produce the life of God when you die and are planted. First Corinthians 15:36 says "...that which thou sowest is not quickened (made alive), except it die...."

Years ago, when archaeologists discovered the tomb of the Egyptian king Tutankhamen, they found kernels of wheat among the artifacts in the burial chamber. They planted some of those seeds and were amazed to find that they still grew after being entombed for thousands of years. There is life-giving power locked up in a seed.

Imagine what God can do with a life that is fully yielded to Him. What kind of harvest is possible if a multitude of seeds are planted, and in losing their lives, they bring forth His life? That is exactly why God has brought us to this place at this time. Our purpose is to bring forth a harvest of souls at the end of the age.

Psalm 126:6 says, "He that goeth forth and weepeth, bearing precious seed, shall doubtless come again with rejoicing, bringing his sheaves with him." Weeping may endure for a night, but joy comes in the morning. Weeping may accompany death and burial, but joy comes with the resurrection of life. It may look barren and bleak when your hopes and dreams are being buried, but the light of His countenance will cause you to rise in victory.

God's purpose for us is not just to be buried in obscurity, but to rise in glory. We are the generation who will come again rejoicing, because of the great harvest that God will bring in at the culmination of all things. The harvest is our purpose, and it starts with a seed.

Psalm 22:30 also says this sacrificial seed shall serve Him—that is, it will fulfill God's purpose. The calling on our lives is worthy of a great purpose, and anything your mind can imagine on its own will be too small. The anointing God has placed within us cannot be constrained by the imagination of men.

Paul had a job to do when he set out on the road to Damascus, and he was convinced he was doing God's will by persecuting the Christians. He had an encounter with God that convinced him otherwise, and his task at the end of the road was completely different than the one he had when he set out. It seems that everyone has a vision these days, but it is only when our vision is cast aside and His vision is accepted that we will find fulfillment and satisfaction. We must learn to love what God loves and hate what God hates.

This is so foreign to the "me first" philosophy that has become a cornerstone of western culture that people who lay down their lives for a cause greater than themselves are labeled as fanatics or extremists. The Bible calls them heroes of the faith.

Jesus said in John 4:34, "My meat is to do the will of him that sent me...." His life was not wrapped up in what He ate or drank, but in doing His Father's will. (Think about this the next time you are tempted to go through the buffet line again.)

Paul described himself in Romans 1:1 as a servant of Jesus Christ. The word servant literally means bondslave—one who serves because of love and not because of necessity. This is the kind of self-sacrificing service that will win a world to Jesus. We have seen every other level of effort, and the results have been sadly disappointing. It's time to do it the way God prescribed.

Finally, Psalm 22:30 declares that this seed shall serve him, and "...it shall be accounted to the

Lord for a generation." If God can get the seed in His hand, the harvest will be assured. In order to understand the certainty with which God speaks here, we must remember the principle of sowing and reaping.

A farmer determines the size of his harvest by the amount of seed he sows. An investor determines his return by the amount of money he invests. The bigger the manufacturing plant, the more products it can produce. Once the seed is in the ground, a harvest is on the way.

We understand that when it comes to sowing natural seed, all kinds of things can happen to threaten the success of the harvest. But this seed is in God's hand and under His divine supervision. There will be no crop failure in this planting cycle, because God Himself is the husbandman.

Micah 2:12-13 says, "I will surely assemble, O Jacob, all of thee; I will surely gather the remnant of Israel; I will put them together as the sheep of Bozrah, as the flock in the midst of their fold: they shall make great noise by reason of the multitude of men. The breaker is come up before them: they have broken up, and have passed through the gate, and are gone out by it: and their king shall pass before them, and the Lord on the head of them."

God is gathering His seed to plant every-where—in the principal cities of nations as well as the highways and byways. His seed is being scattered in places where there is a church on every corner and in places where the gospel has never been proclaimed. You are a part of His gathering, as I am. We are being assembled for one purpose—to bring in a last and final harvest before the glorious appearing of Jesus, our Savior.

Psalm 22:31 proclaims, "They (the seed) shall come, and shall declare his righteousness unto a people that shall be born, that he hath done this." This is not talking about someone else, it is aimed directly at us, the heirs of salvation in this last great act of human drama before the curtain is drawn on this age of human history. As unlikely as it may seem, we are the ones God has chosen to bring forth a spiritual revival leading to moral reformation which will reverberate across the nation and around the world. God is scattering His seed into each sphere of influence in our society— in government, in education, in the arts, sports, and entertainment, in the media, in the family, in business, and in religion.

This righteous, remnant seed is no longer content to stay within the culturally defined constraints of their religious enclaves, but are bursting forth in the power and the anointing of the Holy Ghost into every walk of life. We will not be silent, but we will speak, and not with enticing words of man's wisdom, but with the power and authority of a resurrected Christ. As we do, the sweet influence of the Spirit will invade every area of our culture, and the knowledge of God will cover the earth as the waters cover the sea.

Showtime!

EPILOGUE

It was a time of tremendous moral decline. The standards held by previous generations were eroding, leaving an ethical breach that was flooded with all kinds of vices. New agendas rushed in to fill the void created by discarded tenets of Christian faith that were regarded as outmoded and obsolete. Church membership rolls were increasing, but the spiritual temperature of many in attendance was tepid at best. Science, reason, and the seemingly unlimited capabilities of humanity were exalted above the knowledge of God and His Word.

Reform efforts aimed at cultural leaders bore little fruit. Those in positions of power tipped their hats to religion, but paid little attention as their actions speeded the secularization of society.

Young people, cut adrift from the moorings that held their ancestors steady, found pleasure in new forms of entertainment and clandestine liaisons in out-of-the-way places. The number of unwed pregnancies soared, and time-honored traditions were overthrown.

These were the conditions prevailing in the American Colonies at the close of the 1720s. Who could tell that within a decade, a culture-shaking revival would not only sweep a society, but shape a new nation?

A visiting clergyman with a severe countenance stepped to a pulpit in Enfield, Connecticut on July 8, 1741. Jonathan Edwards read his message, which had been written out in manuscript form, and described in powerful detail the fate of sinners in the hands of an angry God.

"O sinner! Consider the fearful danger you are in: it is a great furnace of wrath, a wide and bottomless pit, full of the fire of wrath, that you are held over in the hand of God…. You hang by a slender thread, with the flames of divine wrath flashing about it, and ready every moment to singe it, and burn it asunder…and [there is] nothing that you have ever done, nothing that you can do, to induce God to spare you one moment."

"Therefore, let every one that is out of Christ, now awake and fly from the wrath to come…. Let every one fly out of Sodom: Haste and escape for your lives, look not behind you, escape to the mountain, lest you be consumed."

And awake they did. They were inspired by the preaching of men like George Whitefield, who covered the colonies preaching from New England to Georgia, attracting crowds of 20,000 or more. Tens of thousands fell to their knees in genuine repentance before the throne of a sovereign and gracious God.

Even as notorious a skeptic as Benjamin Franklin was impressed by the change that was wrought by the revival, which became known as the Great Awakening. Franklin said, "It was wonderful to see the change soon made in the manners of our inhabitants. It seemed as if all the world was growing religious, so that one could not walk through the town in an evening without hearing psalms sung in different families of every street."

After the Revolutionary War, the new nation grappled with establishing a government and securing its borders. The beginning throes of the

Industrial Revolution were beginning to reverberate, and westward expansion across the Appalachians was exploding. The revival that fueled their parents' and grandparents' piety and informed their morality was a distant memory, as men and women focused on a wilderness to be tamed, empires to be built, and money to be made.

In many places, debauchery became the order of the day. By 1810, per capita consumption of hard liquor by those over age 15 was more than seven gallons per year. Entire communities were without one professing Christian. Colleges that had been founded to prepare young men for the ministry had no Christian voice on their entire campuses. Vices that had fallen prey to the great revival of the past once again flourished, not only on the frontier, but in the cities of the east and everywhere in between.

On October 10, 1821, God called a lawyer to plead His case. Charles Grandison Finney was saved in Adams, New York, and within two years had embarked on the most remarkable itinerant ministry of what became known as the Second Great Awakening. With a precision born of a study of law, Finney demolished the arguments of intellectuals and ignorant heathen alike with his preaching. Throughout the cities of western New York, then in urban areas such as Philadelphia and New York City, thousands were convicted and converted to the cause of Christ.

The convicting power of God was so strong that entire communities were changed, not just while the meetings lasted, but for years afterward. In 1830-31 in Rochester, New York, so many in that city were saved, from the mighty halls of power to the merest hut on the edge of town, that according to one observer, "The whole community was stirred. Religion was the topic of conversation in the house, in the shop, in the office and on the street.... Grog shops were closed, the Sabbath was honored, the sanctuaries were thronged with happy worshippers.... There was a wonderful falling off of crime. The courts had little to do, and the jail was nearly empty for years afterward."

In his *Memoirs*, Finney said, "At a subsequent period...I was conversing with a lawyer, who was converted at this revival...and who soon after had been made district attorney of the city…. He said to me, many years afterward: 'I have been examining the records of the criminal courts, and I find this striking fact, that whereas our city has increased since that revival, threefold, there are not one-third as many prosecutions for crime, as there had been up to that time. This is the wonderful influence that revival had upon the community.'"

Conservative estimates indicate that one hundred thousand people began going to church as a result of that one revival, whose effects were felt not only in Rochester itself, but in the surrounding region and beyond. The Second Great Awakening had a similar effect on America as did the first.

I do not need to detail the decline in morality we have seen in America in the past generation, since it is evidently displayed in front of all of us. The lascivious and vile diversions displayed as today's entertainment would make the most blighted rogues of decades past blush with shame. The manmade dogma of humanism, with its foul offspring materialism and hedonism, has become the prevailing religion in America and much of the western world. In our mad rush for self-fulfillment, we are careening close to self-annihilation, as our culture collapses under the weight of our corpulent corruption.

We must have a culture-shaking revolution that comes from a region beyond ourselves that is supernatural in its scope. Our moral compasses must be reset according to a celestial standard that will give us divine guidance in a day of decadence and decay.

These challenges are not unprecedented. Generations ago, our forefathers in the faith contended with entire regions apathetic to spiritual concerns. Like the lepers in the Syrian camp, they had become exhausted with their self indulgence, and were ready to awake to their responsibility before God.

What is it about this generation that will appear different enough to the world to cause them to want what they have? I believe this generation of those who seek God's face will be characterized not only by the power they possess, but by what they are willing to go without. I believe there are at least four characteristics *not* found among this remnant group.

They will not be self-important. Romans 12:3 says, "For I say through the grace of God given unto me, to every man that is among you, not to think of himself more highly than he ought to think; but to think soberly…." Our estimation of ourselves should be based on what God says about us, not on our inflated opinion of ourselves and our abilities. Matthew 23:11 says, "But he that is greatest among you shall be your servant." This is in direct opposition to the spirit of the world which says if you want to be the greatest, you have to advance yourself and belittle everyone else. Jesus said in Luke 9:23, "If any man will come after me, let him deny himself, and take up his cross daily, and follow me." Self-denial is the opposite of worldly prescriptions for success.

They will not be self-sufficient. Matthew 18:18-20 makes it clear that our strength is not in our rugged individualism, but in our sense of community and agreement with each other. Our power is multiplied when we come together, and we are most vulnerable when we are alone.

Without God and without one another, we are like sails without wind, trees without sap, and chariots without steeds. God made us to need one another, and the task we have before us is greater than anyone can accomplish on their own.

They will not be self-willed. "I" and "me" have become the watchwords of the age, as in "I have a right," or "That doesn't work for me." We justify all kinds of iniquity by convincing ourselves that "God wants me to be happy," and we pursue our happiness at others' expense and become more miserable than before. Jesus' prayer was, "Not my will but Thine be done." We must recover this same attitude to experience revival.

They will not be self-indulgent. One of the first questions self-indulgent people ask is, "What's in it for me?" Years ago, the most frequent requests people had when calling our prayer line was for the salvation of their family members. Today, the most frequent request is for their personal healing or prosperity. Salvation for others is well down the list. We must display the same selflessness Jesus demonstrated as He came to give His life, not to save it.

The seed God is gathering together is not self-important, self-sufficient, self-willed, or self-indulgent. It is focused on Him and not self. That seed is a generation that will serve Him, but there is another application.

Psalm 22:30 says, "A seed shall serve him; it shall be accounted to the Lord for a generation." The seed here represents something larger than itself. This is not only talking about a generation God is raising up, it is talking about an actual seed.

Psalm 22 speaks of the Messiah. Jesus Christ is God's ultimate example of a seed. He sowed His life, was buried, and rose again as the first-fruits of a harvest, the culmination of which is yet to be reaped.

God may never require you to give your life by dying on a cross, but He will certainly require other things of you that may appear to be sacrifices. Our lives are a seed in His hand. We spend a portion of our lives; our labor, our time, and our energy working in exchange for money. If our lives belong to God then our money belongs to Him as well. It should come as no surprise that

God will ask you to plant a portion of it into His kingdom to support His purpose. He is asking now. We must respond with obedience.

God is obligated to act according to principles He has outlined in His word. He cannot bring in the harvest of this generation until He has a seed. You cannot reap your harvest until you place a seed in His hand. That seed has to die and be planted. But just as surely as Jesus came out of the tomb, your dead and buried seed will be resurrected into a tremendous harvest.

The amazing thing about the seed God is requiring in this final hour is that this seed represents an entire generation. We are not waiting for another time—this is the time God has ordained to preach the gospel to the ends of the earth. There are multiplied billions still untold, and the curtain is about to close on this drama. We are the actors God has chosen. We have been given a script written by the Holy Spirit, and we have been energized and inspired by the Author Himself. The spotlight is on and the world is waiting.

It's showtime!

About the Author

ROD PARSLEY, bestselling author of more than sixty books, is the dynamic pastor of World Harvest Church in Columbus, Ohio, a church with worldwide ministries and a global outreach. As a highly sought-after crusade and conference speaker whom God has raised up as a prophetic voice to America and the world, Parsley is calling people to Jesus Christ through the good news of the Gospel.

He oversees Bridge of Hope Missions, Harvest Preparatory School, World Harvest Bible College, and the *Breakthrough* broadcast, a television and radio show seen by millions and broadcast to nearly 200 countries around the world, including a potential viewing audience of 97% of the homes in the United States and 78% in Canada. *Breakthrough* is carried on 1,400 stations and cable affiliates, including the Trinity Broadcasting Network, the Canadian Vision Network, Armed Forces Radio and Television Network, and in several countries spanning the globe.

Parsley's refreshingly direct style encourages Christians to examine and eradicate sin from their lives. A fearless champion of living God's way, Parsley follows the high standard set by Jesus Christ and compels his readers to do the same. He and his wife Joni have two children, Ashton and Austin.

OTHER BOOKS BY ROD PARSLEY

Ancient Wells, Living Water

At the Cross, Where Healing Begins

Could It Be?

The Day Before Eternity

He Came First

It's Already There

No Dry Season (Bestseller)

No More Crumbs (Bestseller)

On the Brink (#1 Bestseller)

Repairers of the Breach

Silent No More

For more information about *Breakthrough,*
World Harvest Church, World Harvest Bible
College, Harvest Preparatory School,
The Center for Moral Clarity, or to receive a
product list of the many books, CDs and DVDs
by Rod Parsley, write or call:

Breakthrough/World Harvest Church
P.O. Box 32932
Columbus, OH 43232-0932 USA
(614) 837-1990 (Office)
www.breakthrough.net

World Harvest Bible College
P.O. Box 32901
Columbus, OH 43232-0901 USA
(614) 837-4088
www.worldharvestbiblecollege.org

Harvest Preparatory School
P.O. Box 32903
Columbus, OH 43232-0903 USA
(614) 837-1990
www.harvestprep.org

The Center for Moral Clarity
P.O. Box 32903
Columbus, OH 43232-9926 USA
(613) 382-1188
www.CenterForMoralClarity.net

If you need prayer, Breakthrough Prayer Warriors
are ready to pray with you 24 hours a day, 7 days
a week at: (800) 424-8644